Soulitude

Anu Ghanashyam

Presentation by *BookLeaf Publishing*

Web: www.bookleafpub.com

E-mail: info@bookleafpub.com

ISBN: 9789363318113

First edition 2024

To my mischief-maker a.k.a. best friend, a.k.a. therapist, a.k.a. son Indraneil and my partner-in-everything Ghanashyam,

You two keep life hilariously real and endlessly inspiring.

Your ability to turn every moment into an adventure

keeps me laughing and reaching for the stars.

Thanks for being my constant cheerleaders and co-conspirators.

With all my love and a good dose of chaos,

Anu

ACKNOWLEDGEMENT

Writing 'Soulitude' has been a deeply personal and rewarding journey, and I am immensely grateful to everyone who has supported me along the way.

First and foremost, I extend my heartfelt gratitude to my family. My parents' love and encouragement ignited my creative spark from a tender age. I am equally indebted to my in-laws for their unwavering support and for welcoming me into their family with open arms.

To my beloved husband, Ghanashyam, your steadfast belief in my dreams and your boundless love have been my constant source of strength. You are my inspiration, my confidant, and my rock.

To our extraordinary son, Indraneil, your infectious laughter, brilliant mind, and zest for life are a constant source of joy and wonder. Your spirit inspires me every day.

I am deeply grateful to my cousins, relatives, friends, colleagues, and mentors who affectionately call me "The Laughing Lady."

Your camaraderie, support, and encouragement have been instrumental in bringing these poems to life.

A special thank you to Athulya, Dileep, Lince, Manju, Rakhee, and Rewa for their unwavering belief in me. Your constant support pushed me beyond my perceived limits.

To my readers, your openness to my work and your willingness to share in my emotional journey mean the world to me. Each of you brings a unique perspective to these poems, and I am truly grateful for your connection.

Finally, I would like to express my sincere appreciation to BookLeaf Publishing. The entire team, including the editor, the book designer, and the publishing manager, has been instrumental in transforming my years of writing into a published book. I am truly grateful for your expertise and support.

Thank you all from the bottom of my heart.

With all my love and gratitude,
Anu Ghanashyam

PREFACE

Welcome to 'Soulitude.'

In these poems, I have tried to capture the full spectrum of human life – the quiet moments that soothe the heart, the joyful bursts of success, and the painful struggles we all face. From the peaceful stillness of morning to the loud cheers of victory, these verses explore the feelings that make us human.

Writing them has been a personal journey of self-discovery and connection. Poetry is a way to share our hearts and understand each other better. I hope these poems offer a window into my world, and maybe, you will find a reflection of your own story within them.

Remember those peaceful mornings when the sunrise filled you with a quiet joy? Or those times when laughter with friends was like the best medicine, chasing away all your cares? Remember the times you discovered hidden strength within yourself when facing challenges? Or the pure joy of being reunited with someone you love after being apart? These are the moments I aim to capture in 'Soulitude.'

Thank you for taking the time to read my poems. Forty poems feel like a significant milestone for my first book. This number carries symbolic weight, representing a period of transformation and renewal. It signifies a complete cycle, a journey from one phase to another. I believe it's the perfect number to mark this new beginning.

I hope these words offer you comfort, inspiration, and a sense of connection. Perhaps you will find a piece of yourself reflected in these pages.

With love and gratitude,
Anu Ghanashyam

The Passage of Time

This section offers a chronological exploration of the human life cycle, encompassing the vitality of youth and the profound reflections of later years.

Sprouting Souls

Bare feet on earth, a taste of clay,

A sapling soul, in nature's sway.
Endless days, a dreamy haze,
Tiny hands, in a playful maze.

Down dusty lanes, a barefoot flight,
Swings soaring high, with pure delight.
Monsoon's rhythm, a drumming beat,
Paper boats, a watery fleet.

Skin like clay, soft and warm,
Kites dancing high above the storm.
Innocence blooms, a tender grace,
Thunder's roar, a fearful space.

Growing strong, like roots that bind,
A curious mind, a curious kind.
Childhood's magic, a wondrous spell,
A sapling's story, we know so well.

Ink-Stained Youth

In the depths of a mind, a library lies,

Where shelves overflow and thoughts collide.
Ink-stained fingers dance upon the page,
But words, like whispers, fade with each turning
stage.

A book of life, its chapters yet to unfold,
A curious mind, where stories are told.
Pages filled with questions, doubts, and fears,
A young heart searches through endless years.

The bookmark lost, in chapters gone astray,
An uncertain path, a confusing array.
Identity's quest, a puzzling game,
A character forming a different name.

Hormones storm, like ink on the page,
Emotions wild, a turbulent stage.
Friendships forged, like chapters aligned,
A coming-of-age story, redefined.

The covers close, the book remains unread,
A world unexplored, a heart forever unsaid.
Adolescence, a riddle, a weight to bear,
A tangled plot, a life put to the test with no clear
care.

The Train of Life

Life is a busy train, rushing fast,

People crowding in, a hurried past.
Friendships tangled, like messy string,
Trying to balance everything.

The ride is bumpy, with many a shake,
But holding on tight, for goodness' sake.
Learning to stand, like a steady tree,
Facing challenges, wild and free.

Growing stronger with every mile,
Facing life with a happy smile.
Not just a rider, but the train's heart,
Playing a role, right from the start.

With ups and downs, the journey goes,
Learning and growing as life grows.
A winding path, with many a bend,
A story unfolding, without end.

Silver years

Abanyan tree, weathered by time's hand,

Its roots run deep across the land.
With branches outstretched, a canopy wide,
It bears the weight of years inside.

Wrinkles etched on bark, like life's own art,
A silent story, from the very start.
Leaves turn golden as seasons change,
A gentle cycle without being strange.

Its strength lies not in youth's bold might,
But in the wisdom gathered through light.
It stands as a witness to nature's sway,
A silent teacher, come what may.

Through storms and droughts, it finds a way,
To thrive and flourish, day by day.
A symbol of patience and steadfast grace,
A living legend in time's vast space.

So let us honor, this ancient tree,
A mirror of life, wild and free.
In its wisdom, we find our own,
As life's journey, gently grown.

Symphony

Covering the full range of human emotion, these
18 poems create a unified portrait of the
emotional landscape. Together, they celebrate
the richness and diversity of our emotional lives.

Finding Joy

Sunbeam moments, warm and bright,

A gentle kiss of soft twilight.
A child's laughter, pure and free,
The whispering leaves on a summer tree.

Shared smiles in friendly waves,
The tales we tell, the paths we pave.
A cozy nook, a peaceful night,
A candle's glow, a starry light.

The scent of fresh-baked bread,
The whispered words before we're in bed.
Morning coffee's warming brew,
The skies adorned in every hue.

Music's sweet and gentle flow,
The places where the flowers grow.
To find true joy, we must embrace
Life's simple gifts with heartfelt grace.

Embracing Shadows

Numbness shrouds each step I take,

A shield from feelings, hearts to break.
Wrapped tight against the world's cold grasp,
Inside, a winter's icy clasp.

But here's the truth that I must face,
In darkness, I can find my place.
Amongst the shadows, I seek release,
A moment to breathe, to find my peace.

My loved ones stand with open arms,
Through every storm, through all alarms.
Yet sometimes I retreat alone,
To understand what's not yet known.

In solitude, I find my way,
To overcome, to face each day.
With patience, grace, and gentle care,
I navigate through despair.

Slowly, light begins to mend,
Healing wounds, a steadfast friend.
As shadows soften, hope takes flight,
Painting life with colors bright.

Layers of Love

When skies in gold begin to softly blend,

A canvas painted where soul's stories tend.
Love's gentle touch, a whisper soft and sweet,
Two hearts united, a rhythm pure and fleet.

Love's the path through gardens fair,
A secret bloom we gently share.
In every laugh and tender smile,
Love's the thread that weaves each mile.

Love's the book we read by fire,
A whispered tale of deep desire.
In every glance and touch so close,
Love's the scent of a blooming rose.

Love's the morning's first soft kiss,
A sweet beginning wrapped in bliss.
In moonlit walks and midnight talks,
Love's the rhythm of our walks.

Love's the song we softly sing,
A melody in everything.
Layered deep, with flavors sweet,
Love's the dance where hearts meet.

To keep this love so pure and true,
We cherish moments, old and new.
With souls connected, a perfect art,
Forever joined, heart and heart.

Whispers of Night

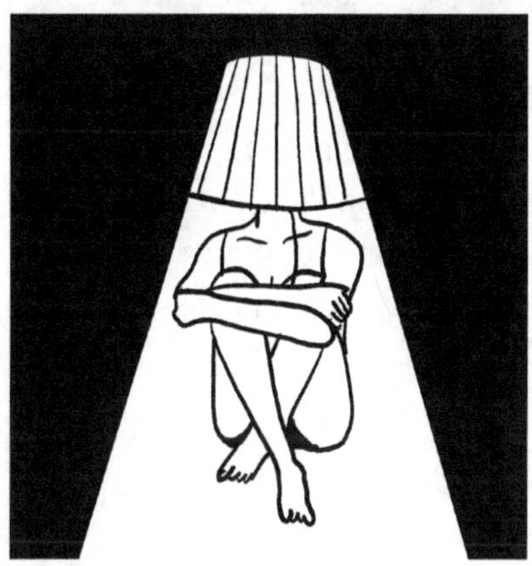

In the garden of my heart, a shadow creeps,

A specter veiled, where the moonlight weeps.
Soft whispers dance on midnight's breeze,
As moonlit shadows sway through trees.

Emotions stir in the moon's uncertain gleam,
Threads of unease weave a haunting theme.
Silence cloaks the velvet dark,
Where thoughts of parting leave their mark.

Amidst fears, a somber mist,
Where doubts of fate softly twist.
Moonlight filters through the misty veil,
Paths where dread's whispers sail.

Yet in the stillness of the moonlit night,
Courage rises to challenge fear's might.
For within each fear, a truth is near,
In moonlit dreams, strength will appear.

Let fears rest in the moon's calming light,
Whispering hope in the deep of night.
In the garden of my soul, truths unfurled,
Love's refuge, where fears are swirled.

Trust the Journey

In doubt's maze and shadows deep,

Vision blurred, where secrets sleep.
Each step, a lesson life reveals,
In joy's touch and chance's wheels.

Navigate the winding path unknown,
Each turn, a chapter yet untold.
Let doubt's mist fade as dawn's light gleams,
Trust your heart, fulfill your dreams.

What seems defeat, life's stormy sea,
Each challenge, a stone, wild and free.
Building strength on life's long path,
A steady soul, a guiding graph.

Let every moment, a cherished pearl be found,
Polished by experience, precious and profound.
In life's grand canvas, colors bright or gray,
We paint our destiny, day by day..

Anger's roar

A storm within, a thunderous sound,

Anger's voice, a challenge profound.
It strikes when hurt, a sudden flare,
Igniting shadows, a darkened sphere.

A force for change, a molten art,
It guides us from life's painful start.
But unleashed a whirlwind's reckless flight,
It leaves destruction, a dimming light.

Contained in a volcano's silent sleep,
A pressure building, depths so deep.
It wears away from within, a steady tide,
Where hope and spirit, wounded and hide.

So let us channel this powerful force,
Transform its rage, a different course.
With a steady hand, we calm the inner sea,
And find a haven where peace can be.
For anger's fire, a double-edged blade,
Can wound or heal, a light or shade.
Let's use its heat to forge a stronger soul,
Where wisdom's glow can make the spirit
whole.

Pride, a golden gift

Pride is the sun that warms the day,

Its golden rays light up our way.
A flower blooming in the spring,
A testament to what we bring.

A mighty oak that stands so tall,
It leaves a whisper to us all.
A river carving through the land,
With pride, we shape and understand.

A rainbow after storms have passed,
A promise that our strength will last.
The stars that twinkle in the night,
Reflect our inner, shining light.

A gentle breeze that lifts our wings,
In pride, our heart's true freedom sings.
A mountain peak kissed by the sky,
With pride, we reach and touch so high.

Pride is the flame that fuels our soul,
A positive force that makes us whole.
It builds us up, it makes us see,
The worth within, our dignity.

Cherish this gift, let it unfold,
A source of warmth, a heart of gold.
With pride as a guide, our spirits soar,
A brighter path forevermore.

Beyond the Cloak

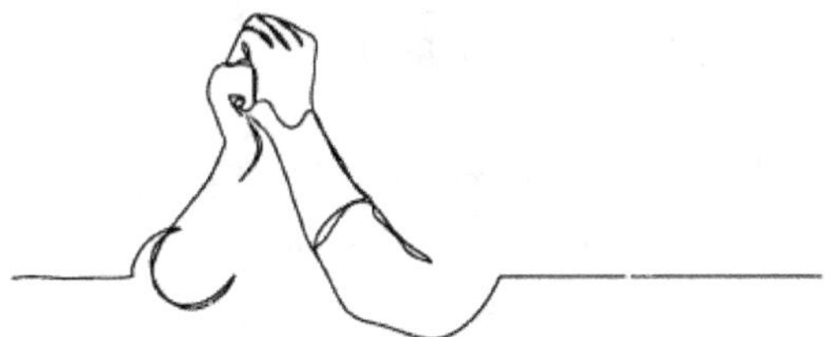

Imagine shame as a heavy cloak,
Draped on the soul, a silent yoke.
For a child, it's a secret fear,
A hidden doubt, a silent tear.

It's the sting of criticism, a gentle nudge,
A quiet worry, a hesitant budge.
The fear of falling, a fleeting phase,
A stepping stone to brighter days.

It's the lonely corner, a moment's pause,
A chance to reflect, to find a cause.
The silent wish, a hopeful spark,
For understanding, a guiding mark.

But healing starts with a helping hand,
A listening ear, across the land.
To share the journey, to lighten the load,
To find strength on life's open road.

For in openness, courage resides,
In shared stories, where spirit guides.
To accept oneself, a beautiful art,
Is to discover a passionate heart.

With kindness sown and hope that grows,
The cloak of shame softly sews.
Transformed to light, a shining ray,
A brighter path, a brand new day.

The Heart of Compassion

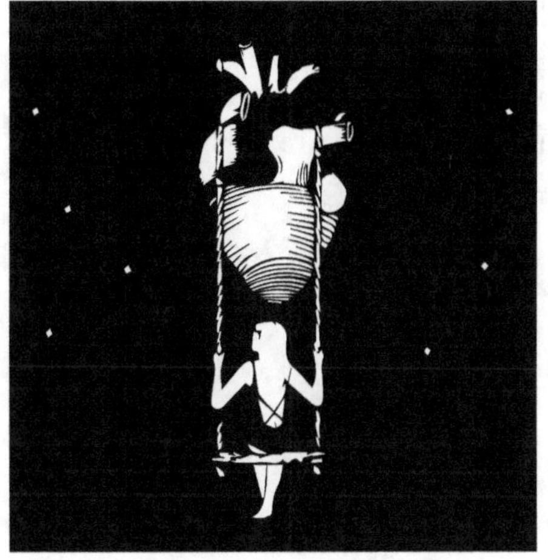

Compassion is at the heart of all we do,

A gentle force, steadfast and true.
The dearest quality we possess,
Yet often lost in life's distress.

In every smile and every tear,
Compassion whispers, "I am here."
A tender touch, a soothing light,
A gentle presence through the night.

Yet, when it's discarded, a mournful refrain
Of bitter regret, echoes through our pain.
To lose our compassion, we lose the key
To what it means to truly be.

For in each act of love and grace,
Compassion finds its rightful place.
A human heart, so warm and kind,
With compassion, we're aligned.

The Forest I Carried

In shadowed woods, I wandered, lost and deep,
A heavy burden, my soul did keep.
Each tree a giant, its branches a cage,
Enclosing my spirit on life's dark stage.

A prisoner of guilt, with chains unseen,
I dragged through the undergrowth, a mournful queen.
The forest's heart echoed with my despair,
As shadows lengthened and hope grew rare.

But dawn approached, dispelling the night's
hold,
And with it, courage – a story untold.
The woods transformed, a path began to gleam,
As I stepped into the sunlight, a hopeful dream.

With newfound freedom, my spirit took flight,
Leaving behind the shadows of the night.
In fields of mercy, where hope does reside,
I found a sanctuary where joy can abide.

No longer bound by darkness, fear, or shame,
I embrace the present, a different game.
With gratitude as my compass, heart aflame,
I navigate life's challenges with a stronger
frame.

And in this journey, I've come to see,
That growth and healing are meant to be.
With every step, I'm reborn anew,
A spirit awakened, with purpose true.

The Gift of Gratitude

When life spins fast and chaos clouds your
view,
Gaze at the sunset's sky, painted with every hue.
Let the colors of dusk bring calm to your mind,
In the celestial dance, peace you'll find.

Feel the earth beneath, as solid as the moon,
Reconnect with its surface beneath the sun's soft
tune.
Thank the air that moves with each breath you
take,
In the cosmic flow, let your spirit awake.

The sun's warm rays can light your weary way,
As stars begin to shine with the close of the day.
In the evening's gentle glow, find your heart's
delight,
Appreciate life's beauty in the fading light.

Gratitude weaves meaning into all we see,
It opens hearts and sets the spirit free.
In moments of stillness, when we pause and
reflect,
We find value in life's simple effects.

So let each sunrise and starry night remind,
To cherish every blessing with a grateful mind.
In life's vast cosmic dance, find joy and grace,
And let your heart be full in this wondrous
space.

The Enchanted Solitude

In quiet moments and nights when
loneliness takes hold,
And shadows whisper tales of hearts grown
cold,
Remember, dear, you're never truly lone,
For magic weaves its threads in ways unknown.

Books will nurture thoughts that softly sing,
Pages turn to worlds where dreams take wing.
Hands can craft and shape, create and play,
Turning solitude into a bright array.

The wind will soothe your soul with gentle
sighs,
A whispered lullaby beneath the skies.
Breaths will calm your nerves with tender ease,
Each exhale brings a sense of peace and ease.

Nature's arms will cradle all your cares,
Soaking worries with the love it shares.
And stars will light your dreams with twinkling
beams,
Guiding you through night's enchanting
schemes.

Though lonely moments come, they too shall
pass,
In solitude, you'll find your strength at last.
For within the quiet, magic lies unseen,
Turning loneliness into a serene dream.

Timeless Summers

I miss those barefoot summer days,

Walking to a friend's house, endless play.
Sweating in the heat, under the scorching sun,
Cycling through dusty lanes till the day was
done.

Climbing neem and mango trees,
Plucking fruits, feeling the breeze.
Mom's call for dinner, the sound so sweet,
Running back home with dusty feet.

We'd rush our meals to reunite,
Swimming in the pond till the moonlight.
Drying our hair by a lantern's glow,
Eating mangoes, laughter's gentle flow.

Back home to bed by nine or so,
Dreaming of adventures, hearts aglow.
Mornings brought the same routine,
Joy unbounded in the summer sheen.

Remember finding sticks in fields,
Transforming them with imagination's yields.
An arrow, sword, or bamboo flute,
A microphone or a cricket bat in pursuit.

A hook to catch dreams from afar,
A slingshot to aim at a distant star.
A flute to play a tune so clear,
A wand for spells, magic sincere.

When monsoon clouds began to form,
Dancing in the rain became the norm.
Puddles splashed, laughter free,
Magic moments, you and me.

The village paths, our endless maze,
Adventures in the summer haze.
With every stick, a new story spun,
Imagination's magic, never done.

Live like there's nothing to lose,
With simple tools, we freely choose.
New beginnings on the village floor,
Adventure awaits, forevermore.

The Jewel of Desire

I've got a thing for those who blaze their
own trail,
Whose messy hair and souls tell a unique tale.
They're the jewels in a world of fleeting gold,
With hearts on their sleeves, they're unashamed
and bold.

Their laughter rings like the finest chime,
In their own success, they find no crime.
Like rarest gems, their passion brightly gleams,
In the fires of their tears flow vivid dreams.

They fight for beliefs with unyielding might,
Their spirits, like diamonds, shine in the night.
In a world of wealth and glittering shows,
Their true worth lies in the love they bestow.

Desire, as an emotion, drives them on,
A force that burns brighter than the dawn.
Their strength remains soft, their fire burns hard,
These are the people who guard my heart's
guard.

For in their light, I see the world anew,
Their fierce, gentle spirits, pure and true.
These are my people, the ones I hold dear,
In their presence, life's riches are clear.

The Tumor of Loss

Your grief is your own, like a tumor that
spreads,
It may surface in moments when you least can
shed.
The loss of a loved one was never planned or
light,
So your sorrow will grow, unyielding in its
might.

You will mourn, you will weep, struggle through
pain,
In moments of silence, where echoes remain.
No need for apologies for the storm you bear,
Grief is a burden you quietly share.

Grief is harsh, a weight that tightens its hold,
A darkening shadow that chills to the cold.
Yet through this struggle, you'll find hearts that care,
Trying to ease the burden you wear.

Though no cure can restore what's lost to the night,
In grief's harsh grip, love still finds its light.
On the other side of this painful design,
You'll find a deep love that helps you align.

The Garden of Forgiveness

In the garden where anger blooms,

We tend to thorns in shadowed rooms.
Each prick of pain, a petal torn,
In the soil of anguish, hearts are worn.

We clutch the stems of past disputes,
Where grudges grow like stubborn roots.
Yet victory in grudge is a fleeting light,
A stubborn dusk that blinds our sight.

Forgiveness is the gentle rain,
That washes grief from every stain.
It's the breeze that lifts the heavy veil,
Turning bitterness into a fragrant trail.

It cannot mend the wounds of yesterday,
Nor erase the pain that still will stay.
Yet, like a garden touched by morning light,
Forgiveness offers hope, a guiding light.

Oceans of Peace

In ocean depths, where waters are calm and clear,
I find a haven, free from harm and fear.
Currents of worry gently wash away,
In soothing tides, my soul learns how to stay.

Stormy waves, I cast aside with ease,
In peaceful depths, my spirit finds its peace.
Negative swells I let slip from my grasp,
In ocean's shelter, my burdens unclasp.

And then it happens, dolphins glide with grace,
You find a world where joy lights every place.
Your heart is calm, your soul begins to glow,
With dolphins' dance, your thoughts start to flow.

At peace with where you've been, the past is
gone,
With what you've faced and all you've known.
In this vast sea, your joy is forever drawn,
A boundless horizon, where new hopes dawn.

The Spectrum of Life

From birth's first cry to life's final bow,

A vibrant circus, the soul's grand show.
Joy's confetti dances, a playful cheer,
Fear's dark shadow, a haunting sphere.

Love's sweet candy, a cherished delight,
Anger's fury, a blinding light.
Hope's carousel, spinning dreams so high,
Despair's lone clown, a tearful cry.

Ambition's tightrope, a daring feat,
Compassion's gentle touch, a sweet retreat.
Nostalgia's mirror, reflecting years gone by,
Wisdom's stage, where lessons lie.

Loss's somber tent, where grief resides,
Peace, the final curtain, where spirit hides.
A wondrous spectacle, life's colorful show,
With every moment, a lesson to know.

As the curtain falls on life's grand stage,
We carry memories, a cherished page.

Wandering Whispers

This collection captures random thoughts and musings. These poems explore fleeting, imaginative, and meaningful moments. They offer a glimpse into the poet's contemplative and creative mind. This section invites readers to ponder and wander through various reflections.

Her Survival

Each day and night, she inhales the air,

Racing 'gainst time, for a life more fair.
A role to play, a mask to wear,
To fit reality without a care.
But wicked thoughts, a tangled snare,
Confine her spirit, in deep despair.

The game began in ages past,
For this world's pace, too swift and fast.
Her wings clipped, grounded, alas,
Yet, stories untold, a valiant mass.
Endurance tested, a silent plea,
For stronger bonds, wild and free.
A quest for courage, to rise and strive,
To live and breathe, and truly thrive.

Sweetest Longing

A caramel dream, a honeyed art,

Love, a sweet nectar, close to my heart.
A chocolate craving, a sugary yearn,
For your embrace, where passions burn.
A vanilla kiss, a soft caress,
Your love, a dessert in sweet excess.
A cupcake craving, a longing deep,
For your warm smile, my soul to keep.
A candy heart, with flavors so true,
Our love story, ever new.
A sugar rush, a sweet delight,
In your loving arms, day and night.
A caramel swirl, our hearts aligned,
Love's sweetest melody, a peaceful mind.

A chocolate truffle, rich and deep,
Our love's essence, a treasure to keep.
So let us savor this love so sweet,
A perfect blend, a blissful retreat.
In this confection, our hearts agree,
Eternally bound, you and me.

The Rose's Final Bloom

Death's shadow, a chilling, mournful rose,

Whose thorns pierce deep, where sorrow grows.
A fragrant bloom, yet petals tinged with fear,
A haunting whisper in the mortal sphere.

The unknown garden, where shadows creep,
A silent terror, where memories sleep.
To leave behind this world, so warm and bright,
A chilling prospect in the fading light.

We fear the pain, the tears that will cascade,
For loved ones left, in sorrow's shade.
A heart divided by love and dread,
As life's sweet chapter draws to its head.

But know, dear soul, you're not alone at night,
For every life, a fading, twilight light.
We share this journey; hand in hand, we roam,
Towards that final, undiscovered home.

Though fear may linger, like a haunting chime,
Cherish the present in this precious time.
For in each moment, beauty can be found,
A garden blooming on sacred ground.

And when the petals fall and life is done,
Our essence lingers like the setting sun.
In the hearts of loved ones, memories reside,
A fragrant echo, where spirits reside.

So let us cherish every fleeting breath,
And face the unknown with courage, not death.
For in this journey, lessons we will find,
A soul's true purpose, peaceful and resigned.

Reflections

You stood upon the brink of my life,
And at the tip, you left yourself to strive.
I wonder how and why,
Because with a smiling face,
I hear you cry!
You shout all agony with your eyes,
Leading many around you – Jeopardize!
When will you let yourself be free,
Because that's when happiness guarantees,
Clutches of thoughts will bury,
All that which was once merry,
Shred off all those worries,
Don't let yourself live eerie!
Because beautiful are those eyes and smiles,
Let it be meaningful from far miles and miles!

Water's Whisper

Starting as a slender stream, she conquered
hills and valleys,
Leaving her imprint on every rock she passed
with such ease,
She encountered countless rivers, sharing her
oceanic dream!
All yearned for the sea, the mighty, boundless
sea!

Thousands cleansed themselves within her pure
flow,
Her innocence and integrity, a pristine glow.
Humanity's currents, often tainted and deep,
As desires and lustful ambitions, their waters
steep.

Carefree at first, she followed nature's art,
Exploring freely with a joyful heart.
But slowly, her path became obscured and slow,
Her once clear waters, now a murky show.

Yearning to regain her pristine, sparkling grace,
She awaits the rain's rejuvenating embrace.
A rainbow's promise, to restore her light,
And reach the ocean with renewed might.
Even a fleeting glimpse, a final art,
To fulfill her journey from the very start.

Empty Spaces

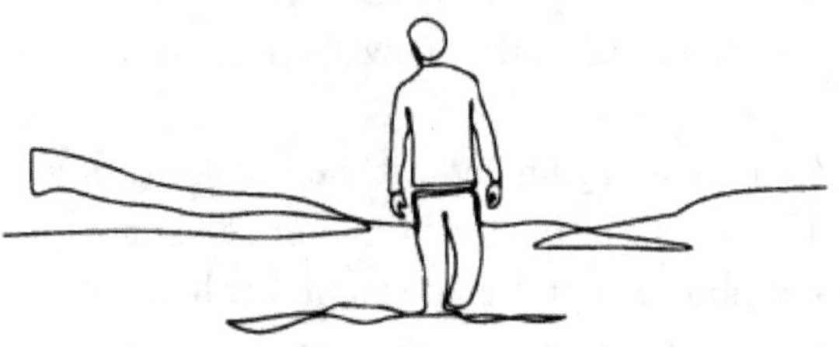

Emptiness, a void, a chasm deep,

Where shadows dwell and sorrows seep.
A barren land, devoid of life's sweet art,
A vacant space, a broken heart.

Once filled with sunshine, laughter's glee,
Now desolate, a barren sea.
A soul once vibrant, now forlorn and gray,
In emptiness's cold grip, it fades away.

A phantom thief that steals our light,
And shrouds our world in endless nights.
A heavy burden, hard to bear,
A lonely exile in despair.

But in this darkness, hope may reside,
A flicker of light, a guiding tide.
To fill this void with love and grace,
And find a sanctuary, a peaceful place.

For in this emptiness, we can create,
A masterpiece of hope, a joyous fate.
To plant new seeds where sorrow grew,
And watch our spirits, strong and new.

Lost in Echoes

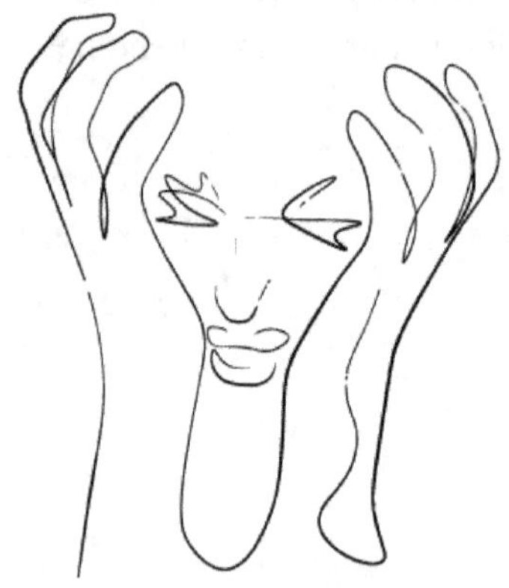

Where do I turn when lost and alone,

Seeking peace, a heart turned to stone?
Yearning for quiet, a retreat from strife,
But echoes of silence, a stagnant life.

I laugh through tears, a painful disguise,
While locked doors mock my desperate cries,
Will this solitude forever reside,
A haunting companion, where shadows hide.

I glimpse a connection, a fleeting grace,
But voices are distant in an empty space.
Reaching out, hands extended, a futile plea,
As hope dissolves, like morning rain.

Coldness creeps in, a chilling emptiness,
As loved ones' shadows vanish in stillness.
Forgotten whispers, a haunting sound,
A soul adrift, in depths profound.

This loneliness, a suffocating sea,
Drowning my spirit, wild and free.
But in the depths, a flicker of hope,
To rise and conquer life's endless scope.

Finding the Core

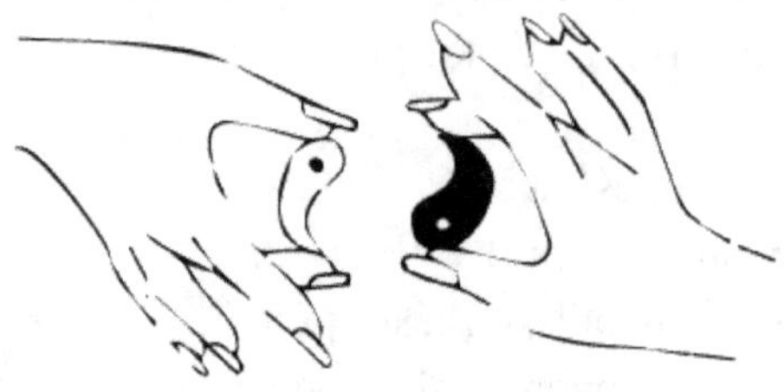

Positivity, a gem to find,

Within your heart, a treasure mined.
Like bees that buzz with joyful glee,
Discover happiness, wild and free.

A choice to make, a path to tread,
To view life's twists as seeds are spread.
With every turn, a lesson's sown,
A garden grows where joy is known.

So why this zest, this buoyant cheer?
Through trials and triumphs, spirit is clear.
Each moment, a canvas, fresh and new,
A blessed life, a hopeful view.

Laughter's gift, a priceless art,
A healing balm to mend the heart.
Choose sunshine over stormy skies,
Let inner light, a steady flame arise.

External joys, like fleeting dreams,
Internal light forever gleams.
A core of strength, a steady flame,
Igniting passion, without blame.

Sunlight of Soul

My heart, a hummingbird, seeks joy's
bloom,
Beside me, daffodils in a sunny room.
A promise of rain, my spirit can sense,
While others bask in carefree pretense.

A lunatic, they brand, with careless haste,
But wisdom's found in life's steady pace.
This brightness, a mere mimicry of cheer,
True joy resides when spirits are clear.

In quiet moments, when the world is still,
The soul awakens with a stronger will.
To peel back layers and truly see,
The essence of life, wild and free.

Let's seize this light, this sun-kissed art,
And nurture happiness deep in the heart.
With spirit as guide and soul's flight,
We'll find true joy, a radiant light.

Harmony Beyond the Grind

In life's relentless race, a weary grind,

Our souls are captive, hearts left behind.
Bound by duty, in shadows we dwell,
Ignoring the whispers, a soulful spell.

But time, a thief, steals moments of grace,
For passions to flourish, a needed space.
Let's break free from life's rigid chain,
Embrace the self and soothe the pain.

In quietude, find inner peace,
Let worries fade and tensions cease.
For balance is key, a gentle art,
To heal the soul and mend the heart.

In nature's embrace, let the spirit soar,
Discover passions to explore.
For life's true colors, vibrant and bright,
Shine in the darkness, a hopeful light.

Lift the Fog

In shadows deep, where worries reside,

A heart lost wandering, unsure guide.
A simple question, a friendly touch,
Can mend the spirit and heal so much.

When skies are gray and hope is dim,
A listening ear, a comforting hymn.
Share your burdens without fear,
A friend's support can bring you cheer.

Together, we'll weather life's storm,
With open hearts, keeping you warm.
In this journey, we're never alone,
Our spirits connected – a heart's own zone.

So let us lift the fog and find the sun,
With empathy and love, as one.
For in this world, where shadows creep,
Human kindness, our souls will keep.

It's Okay to Crumble

You don't have to wear a mask of strength,
Or hide your feelings at every length.
It's okay to feel, to break, to mend,
A human heart, a faithful friend.

Let emotions flow, wild and free,
Scream, cry, or curse authentically.
The sky weeps rain yet shines so bright,
We too can weather, any night.

It's okay to fall, to lose your way,
To rise again, a brighter day.
For in our cracks, new life can start,
A healed heart, a stronger part.

So let it out – the pain, the fear,
Face the darkness, disappear.
In shadows deep, find inner light,
To rise above with all your might.

With time as healer, wounds will mend,
A stronger spirit, to ascend.
So let go gently, let your soul soar,
Discover strength, forevermore.

Journey of Growth

Beneath the sun's warm, golden beams,

A mango tree once planted dreams.
In storms of life, its branches bent,
Through trials faced, its strength was spent.

Its leaves would tremble in the breeze,
Yet roots grew deep beneath the seas.
With time, it stood so tall and strong,
A testament to right and wrong.

Heartaches once so sharp and keen,
Like whispers now in twilight's sheen.
The scars remain, but now they tell
Of battles fought and standing well.

Each season passed, the tree did know,
That from each tear, it learned to grow.
Its fruits, so sweet, with memories blend,
Of times once dark, now on the mend.

In laughter, in the morning light,
The mango tree regained its sight.
It flourished, blooming, proud, and free,
A symbol of resilience, see.

For though the past still lingers near,
The future's path is bright and clear.
We learn, we change, and we bestow
The wisdom gained from seeds we sow.

So stand beneath the mango's shade,
Feel peace where once fear was displayed.
We grow, we heal, we rise anew,
Like mango trees in morning dew.

When will the Sun shine?

Why does it always happen to me,

The storms that rage, the troubles that be?
Why can't the sun just shine through,
Bringing a brighter, hopeful view?
Surrender now, the voice does say,
Let go of worries, come what may.
We can't control life's winding path,
Nor the trials that seem to last.
Why do good things always delay?
Why can't I find a brighter day?
Release the need to steer your fate,
Trust in time, and calmly wait.
One day you'll look back and see,
The reasons for your misery.
Through tears and cries, you'll understand,
Why things didn't go as planned.

More Than Mountains

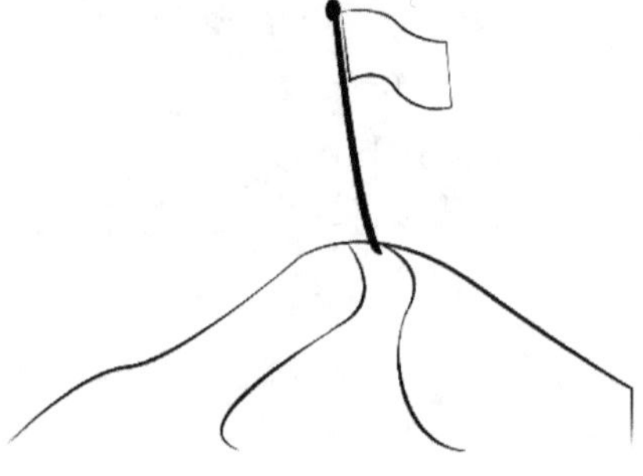

You are more than the valleys of doubt,
More than the echoes of past mistakes,
You are the mountain, solid and strong,
Carved by the winds, yet standing tall.

Dreams linger in your heart like stars,
Guiding you to peaks only you can reach,
The summit whispers your name alone,
No need to compare, no need to compete.

Your journey is carved in the rock,
By hands unseen but always there,
Every stumble, every fall,
Is just a step in your ascent.

Let go of the voices that tether you down,
Trust in the climb, trust in the strength,
For you were made to conquer these heights,
To love, to inspire, to leave your mark.

You are the mountain and the climber too,
Strong enough to rise, to leap, to fly,
Your story is just beginning to unfold,
And you are worthy of every peak, every sky.

Believe it, for the mountain within you,
Is destined to touch the heavens above.

The Playground Within

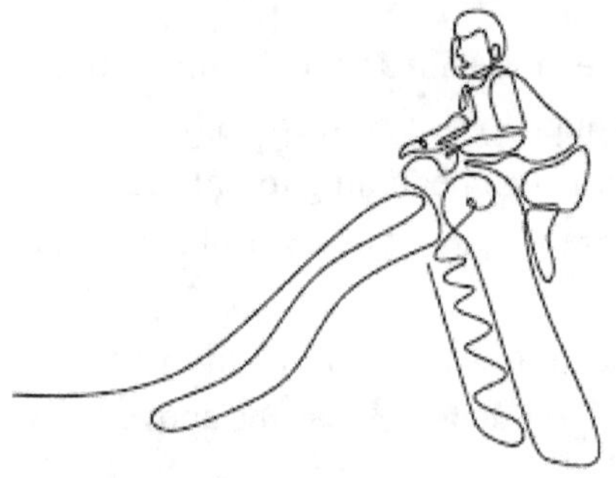

In the sandbox of the soul,

where dreams are made of clay,
you dig with hands so gentle,
and mold the light of day.

You sit beneath the shady tree,
where secrets softly lie,
and in the whispers of the leaves,
you find out how to fly.

The swing set holds your hopes and fears,
you push, you pull, you glide,
and every swing, a question asked,
reveals the spark inside.

You learn to skip on cobblestone,
each step a simple truth,
and in the hopscotch of the heart,
you rediscover youth.

The see-saw of your thoughts,
rises, falls, then soars,
you balance out the highs and lows,
and open hidden doors.

You build your castles in the sand,
and watch them wash away,
but in the act of letting go,
you find a brighter day.

So stay within this playground,
with every scar and smile,
for in the childlike innocence,
you learn to love your style.

You dig, you dream, you question,
you play until you see,
that who you are is beautiful,
just as you were meant to be.

The Chessboard of Self

On the chessboard of your soul,

you move with cautious grace,
but saying "yes" when you mean "no,"
is losing in this race.

You apologize to those who owe,
their words of guilt to you,
but every piece you sacrifice,
is a part of you that's true.

You dig your heels in deeper still,
when wrongness fills your side,
ignoring that the move you made
should've been cast aside.

You explain your truth to silent ears,
a rook against the wall,
but in this game, the barest move
shouldn't be your call.

You chase the knights who flee from you,
their armor shining bright,
yet all they leave are empty squares,
where you stood firm in fight.

You build a life of polished wood,
a king upon his throne,
but every move you make for looks,
leaves the heart alone.

You bend and twist to fit the mold,
in castles made of sand,
ignoring that your intuition
should be your guiding hand.

You stay within a game long played,
a queen with power lost,
not seeing that the time has come,
to count the final cost.

You run on fumes, you skip your rest,
a pawn that's pushed too far,
staying quiet when disrespected,
like a dimming star.

You lie to self, refuse the help,
that could reset the board,
never risking, never living,

like a knight without a sword.

You celebrate the hollow wins,
of those who merely play,
wishing you were someone else,
on a distant, brighter day.

But on this chessboard, know your worth,
each piece, each move, your own,
and when you play with self-respect,
your victory is shown.

The Enigma of Existence

A solitary poem exploring life's questions. It offers a philosophical contemplation of our purpose and place in the world, serving as the conclusion to the collection.

Seed's Purpose

Life's a puzzle, pieces scattered wide,

A story unfolding, where dreams reside.
We're seeds that sprout, with roots so deep,
Growing stronger while memories sleep.

Like ocean waves, we rise and fall,
Learning lessons, answering life's call.
Connected souls, in this world we share,
Kindness echoes in the stillest air.

Be a friend, a helping hand,
In this world, we all understand.
Let your spirit soar, like a bird in flight,
Facing challenges with all your might.

With every step, a chance to mend,
A beautiful journey without end.
Growing stronger with each new day,
Finding your path, come what may.